A PRODIGAL'S DIARY

My Journey back to God

GARY COWIE

Main translation in use: The Message Bible

Published by
Maurice Wylie Media
Your Inspirational Christian Publisher

Publishers' statement: Throughout this book the love for our God is such that whenever we refer to Him, we honour with Capitals. On the other hand, when referring to the devil, we refuse to acknowledge him with any honour to the point of violating grammatical rule and withholding capitalisation.

For more information visit
www.MauriceWylieMedia.com

Contents   Page

Dedication

I would like to dedicate this short book to my parents: a father who is everything he needs to be; who is a man I would love to be like; and a mother filled with love, humility and selflessness. No better parents could anyone hope for.

Introduction

At times in our lives we feel detached, powerless and maybe even worthless. We think we have wandered too far. It was never deliberate, but it happened. God seems distant, disengaged and uninterested; but we simply trudge on. We know where we should be; but the pain to get there is frightening and puts most of us off.

This short story is the ultimate journey of discovery: not self-discovery, but a journey of knowledge, realism and hope. God has always been there. He has been waiting for us to come to our senses and return to Him. This story is for all those who feel they are beyond redemption; too far away; too entrenched; too unworthy; or too hurt. God restores. God forgives. God loves us unconditionally. This is the most momentous story of restoration. We are never out of His reach; never beyond forgiveness; and never unusable.

It is time to come home.

Time to be part of the family again.

Time to be loved.

Time to be accepted.

Time to be who we were created to be.

CHAPTER 1
Brought to my senses

So, I am sitting here on the rocks; literally and metaphorically. I am lost. As I look back over the past years, reality hits, and it hits hard. I am not the man I want to be. I have known it for years and wanted to do something about it, but life got in the way. I have withdrawn myself; have hidden from close encounters with people, even those I care about. I have buried myself in work. I am not the man I should be.

Sin has corrupted me for years. If I am honest, I have had a foot in both camps. I have presented a reasonable image to the world; but with a hollow heart. I have tried to just cope; to push the pain downwards; to make it through. My sins are many: some large, some small. Yet, when I am alone, they present themselves to me time and time again. Sometimes, I am overwhelmed, almost paralysed by fear. The past haunts me. The present concerns me. The future I want to run from.

I wear the mask well. I can even judge and pass comment on others who have failed. I can say the right things at the right time, so I can pass myself in any circle. I may not be living wildly at this moment, but I am suffering from past mistakes. I struggle at times to even lift my head. Fear surrounds me; guilt eats away at me. The weight of my sin is unbearable.

I look around, and everyone seems to have it together: new jobs, progress and excitement. Everyone's life seems better than mine. Perspective is lost, and all that I have achieved seems modest in comparison to others. I am not living the life I want to be living, nor am I giving my family the life I want to give them. I robbed them of who I should be a long time ago, and have almost lost the idea of who I aspired to be.

If only people knew what I was really like: for once could I take off the mask; and then comes the big question... could I cope with the shame and regret, or the disappointment when I consider everything I was and could have been? I feel I have strayed too far, having untied the rope and drifted. I did not set out to travel this far; in addition to the distance, so much time has passed. I was once young and wanted to change the world; now I have concluded that the world changed me. I am what I did not want to be.

So here am I in a place I don't want to be; in a place that I know God would not want me to be... I'm feeding slop to the pigs. I wish I could blame people for my choices, but, maybe for the first time, I admit I have chosen this journey. It was me, the selfish one, who chose to go my own way. I projected to people and to myself that I was somehow content in the emptiness. I took the inheritance that God had given and misspent it. I find it difficult to say, out of shame; but I let Him down; I failed Him. I don't just think I humiliated Him; I know I did. How could He even want to mention my name? I am at the bottom, hitting rock; no farther can I go. God must be ashamed of me; of what I have taken from Him and how I have used it: the wasted hours; the unused gifts; the thankless heart. Through all the brash arrogance of selfish living, I was meant to be someone else. I was meant to carry the family name into all the world; to live an upright life; and to make Him proud. At least, that's what I thought.

No-one needs to tell me where I am: I know I am lost. I know the pain I must be causing Him in rejecting Him. Having chosen myself, I lost sight of Him; so I see Him weaving through my life. All I see is me: my sin, my wrong choices, my shame, my guilt, my regret, and my fear. I hide from those who would make me accountable. I stumbled often. Even though I hated that life, I still went back daily. I knew who I was supposed to be. I knew what my purpose was. I knew whose I was. Yet, I still needed to do it my way. Look how that has turned out! Feeding pigs.

But still, my hunger remains: that desire to be with Him; to go to Him; to fall at His feet and just beg. Is there hope? I look at the pods and the pigs and long for more than this. He owes me nothing. Is that man still inside, deep down? Is there still a chance that all this could be turned around?

The enemy tells me I am worthless. He tells me loudly and openly that I have gone too far. I cannot go back to the start. The enemy tells me I am too far-gone to be restored: I am too dirty. The life that I have lived, and the shame, have made me irredeemable. How could He want me now? Surely, He does not want my shame. My sin is too big. He only wants good people. He does not want the hypocrite that I have become. I am sure He cannot even look at me. I can see His face now: the tears of disappointment, the look of regret, and the shame of once calling me His son.

I already said it: He owes me nothing. He brought me into this world; set my path, educated me. He brought me into His loving family; and picked me up when I fell. He was always there, providing everything a child needed. He showed me love; patience, joy, and just kept giving me more of Him. What was my response? 'Give me what is mine', even though I have not earned it. I did not work hard. I was simply thinking of me. How rejected must He feel? I turned my back on Him to run to this life. I fled fulness for this? He built up the family silver; He did all the work, while I felt entitled. It was mine, right? He did not get me; He did not understand what the world offers; He should have listened to me. I had to taste and see what was outside our home. My agenda; my plan, my timetable, were what was important. I knew better – didn't I?

There I was loved. I did not have to try to be someone else; I was accepted for who I was. The times He picked me up when I fell. How He gently knelt by me to wipe my tears away. Each scar I have reminds me of a story. Each story is about His love, His care and His healing. He was always there; always loving, and never judged. I just took it all for granted. Why did I resent the life He had built for me? Why did I turn my back on Him? I rebelled. I chose to turn my back.

Why can't I just forget Him? Every day I think about home. The longer I stay here, the louder the Voice inside says, 'Go home'. But it is too late, isn't it? He would not want to know me; not after all this. Nothing is hidden from Him. I am sure He knows all I have done. The times He has had to cover His ears as others have told Him of my sin; or covered His eyes as He sees the stories; the shame He must feel. This is it, then. I am stuck here with the pigs; although I cannot quieten this yearning to go to Him. I feel a warmth when

I consider home. I want to be a man after His own heart. I want to change the world with Him; but I am sure He has moved on. I am too dirty. I am too far away.

CHAPTER 2

The giants I cannot slay

What if I were considering going back to Him? I have huge giants that I cannot overcome. They dominate my days (and nights!). They are the sins I grapple with; addictions I easily return to; doubts, fears, the giants are everywhere. They pervade all my thinking: even when I cast a momentary smile, fear rushes in. Surely, I need to beat them before I ever think about going back to Him? He would not accept me in this state. I am far from the man I want to be, and I live on the fringes. After any 'success' I achieve, the joy is quickly stolen from me as the enemy whispers about those moments. The enemy persuades me that I will never be good enough. My sins are too many; the giants are too big; Father would not want to use me again. In reality, He probably could not use me again. I have broken so much of His Word. I never willingly set out to do so; I just got lost along the way. There was no conscious effort to stray: it just happened. Now I am so far away that I cannot even see the shore.

Let me think about the giants for a moment. I have heard people say that life is too short for regrets, but I am forced to disagree. I regret many things; for example, shame weighs heavy upon me, and in this respect, I doubt I will ever get over my past. The enemy uses the guilt I feel over past sins to keep me down. I was going to say 'past mistakes'; but honestly, they are bigger. The word 'mistakes' would be just to ease my conscience because it was my choice to disobey. We cannot deny the fact that sin is open rebellion. At that moment, I chose to turn my back on God. When I consider the people I have let down; God's Word which I disregarded; the punishment due for my choices; and most of all, a disappointed God – I freeze. The things my eyes have seen do not bear repeating

Fear is another giant, based on the question "what if God rejects me?" I hear the phrase "Not everyone who says *'Lord, Lord....*',[1] and am haunted by that statement. If I have gone too far, there is no way back, and the condemnation of people would be unbearable. If I did return, how would my brother feel, and how would those in the family react? Would they retreat into piety and judgement, or step up to grace and forgiveness? Sadly, really, I do not know. In my deepest, darkest hours, I do not see my family here. I am alone, and time has aged me. I have lost my place in the world, and in the family. Sadly, there seems to be no search party. Does this family really just bury its wounded? Fear

---

[1] Matthew 7:22

leads me to jump to inconceivable conclusions (2+2 is 7). Am I the only one? Is there anyone worse than me? Is there anyone who has been restored; truly restored?

I just keep stumbling along. I keep coming back to feed the pigs. I am jealous of them: their life is simple. They may be dirty and smelly, but they are worth something: worth enough for someone to give me the job of feeding them. They wait to be fed. As I watch, all the time, there is a growing aching within me. I know I am not who I should be; nor am I who I want to be. What if I go back to Him? Do I dare believe this glimmer of hope in my heart? Is there really complete forgiveness? Complete restoration into the family?

I am tired; tiredness leads to resentment; resentment leads to blame. The enemy accepts the open door and sympathises with me. He tells me to take my eye off the guilt and self-condemnation. He points me gently towards how I have been rejected. He moves the glare of accountability. Well, he can try; I know who is to blame: me. I chose; I fell; I walked further and further away. I ended up here in this pigsty because of me. Maybe the enemy is right though; the giants are too big? Shame, guilt, fear and worthlessness, all go before me; constantly dwell with me; and follow my every thought or action. Am I really beyond forgiveness? Does my Father really want a life without me? Is He better off without me in the family? Does He care?

CHAPTER 3

Just desserts

I am hungry. Even the servants that work for my Father are in a better position. They are looked after by Him. What am I doing here? I need to go home – back to my Father. I can either wallow around this pigsty and live with these pigs as companions, longing for a break, for my luck to change; or I can 'man up' and go back home.

It is now a wrestle with a new giant called pride. I know what I need to do: humble myself and admit that I am to blame. I need to accept the blame for my situation. I am starving in a pigsty; directionless, empty, lonely. The people I relied on are gone. I had nothing to offer them, so they left. I derived my sense of purpose from others, by trying to make everyone happy; but I wasted my time, my money, and my emotion. Those people were fair-weather friends, in my life for only a season; a very damaging season. I chose my friends badly: they contributed to the pull away from God. Not one of them challenged me about how I treated my Father. Not one encouraged me to make things right. Living was fun; but it was always going to end. Living for myself, I ignored the signs. Anything that I did not enjoy, I removed;

stepping away from accountability. I chose my new life; the new friends were an accessory. Now I am living in my just desserts. I rejected, and now I have been rejected. This is an inevitable circle of life. Pride stops me from being real: just hoping it will all blow over, and a new way will open. Pride casts partial blame on Him; on them. Pride excuses me, and tells me I am the victim.

Yet… I have a list of wants, which are no longer inward-looking. I want to overcome, I want these giants to fall, I want to get right with my Father. Yes, I want to be at home; I need to be cared for, to have a purpose; but these will not satisfy. I want restoration into what is lasting. I want the relationship back with my Father. I want Him in my life. I want to be held accountable. But… I deserve punishment, and to be rejected. How can I stand before my Father and look Him in the eye? I am ashamed of who I have become. Is He really for me? I have made my mind up: I am going home. However long that takes, I am determined to get there.

I will admit I was wrong, and will own my sin. After all, I was the active party: I chose to disobey, and ultimately to walk away. I allowed the bright lights to dazzle me. I even forced my Father to give me my inheritance ahead of time. I stopped engaging with Him: stopped listening, stopped talking to Him. I rejected my home and family, and allowed the relationship with Him to fall apart. Look where that got me. I am going to look my Father in the eyes and apologise. Sorry is the only word I can say. I cannot make up for the past or put it in order. I cannot cover the sin; cannot correct my mistakes. I cannot unhurt those I have hurt; cannot take back those words or refuse to act as I did. I sinned and am worthless. I am no longer Your son. I lost that entitlement when I rejected You. I am wholeheartedly sorry, and I long to change. I want to be different. Yes, my situation is dire, but I am the problem.

I have no rights. I would not even dream of asking for anything. I will beg for a job. I will show Him how I am serious about change. I will prove to my Father that I can work hard. I am no better than His workers. In fact, if truth be told, I am worse. I need a purpose that is not about me. I need to feel valued in the right way. He will see me work long hours. I will show Him my sincerity and take whatever punishment due. I will not argue. I am the guilty party. Whatever He says, I will do. I will tear down these walls: I am determined. Is there a chance that I can feel value again? I am not looking for blessing, just forgiveness, acceptance, and to accept my fate. He is innocent, and I hurt Him. I want to show Him that my stubbornness has been torn apart by guilt. What if He rejects me? What if I am dead to Him? What if I confess and beg for mercy, and it does not come? He does not owe me anything. I must do my part: acknowledge my guilt, own my sin. I must repent and ask for forgiveness. I must put right the offence, all because I just want to be there: to be home with my Father. I want to feel loved and secure. Nothing else will do. Why am I still here? What is stopping me leaving?

CHAPTER 4

The Walk home

I quit. I left the pigsty and have now officially turned my back on my past life. I know I have tried before – in fact, I had tried many times to leave it, only to be sucked back when I faced adversity. Leaving behind the past, and more pointedly, the sins of the past, is only the first step towards restoration. I feel excited. I have not felt like this for a long time. Normally, a smile is wiped away by regret. I have spent so long in the trenches; so long battling, that I have become hardened. I used to shed a tear at beautiful moments: movies, stories, memories; but lately, those tears have dried up. Guilt has fuelled every motivation to get up in the morning.

I am in a positive mood! I am walking back to Him. I am determined to be able to free myself from this life; to remove the shackles of despair; to lift my head, to smile, to laugh, with no fear of repercussion. I just want to be there. Nothing else will do. The journey is ahead of me, but I have taken the first step. I have turned towards Him, facing home. Hope has appeared on the horizon. I have not experienced this feeling in such a long time. Already I know what I need to say. I am ready to humble myself; to acknowledge my sin.

I am ready to open up my heart: I just want to be in His presence. I do not want blessing; only to be right with Him. Maybe He can even use me in the future. Who knows?

As I take step after step walking across all kinds of terrain, the enemy attacks, and I am suddenly conflicted. My joy is being robbed. Fear and hope are mixed. Will He accept me? Have I gone too far? The enemy is subtle and devious. He seeks to plant a small seed of doubt in my mind, encouraging me to allow it to grow into a seemingly impossible obstacle. He tells me of the coming rejection, and reminds me of the shame. I feel it rise within: each step becomes difficult; breathing is increasing, heart beating faster. I feel anxious, tired, unrested. The momentary elation has been replaced by despair. I was hopeful, but am back to focusing on the problems, and I lose sight of Him. But this time is different. I am not looking back. I am not returning to the slop. My desire to be with Him is the only thing that matters. I want to simply be caught up with Him; to feel His presence so deeply that I am transfixed. To know Him; to feel that touch which will never leave me.

As I walk, I go from the highs to lows and then back to the highs before collapsing again to the depths. Everything must change. Everything will change. I need everything to change. I want everything to change. Restoration with Him is all I long for: to have my Father back again, and to be with Him.

What will everyone think of me when I arrive through the gates? The fear of their judgement is overwhelming. Can I cope with the knowing looks, the sly comments, the whispering, and the hostility? I have let more than my Father down. I am determined to show them all I want to change. I do have a good heart. Maybe the evidence of my lifestyle does not reflect it, but I do genuinely love people. I care, and give love to people. I give time, and I give of myself. I just want one last chance to show that I can be His. I know I am in the gutter, but if anyone can lift me up, it is my Father. There is no one else who can do it. I am alone: completely alone; except for my Father. He is my last hope, my only hope. I am energised as I trudge home. My life is about to change. I will offer Him all of me, everything, nothing withheld. He owes me nothing.

CHAPTER 5

What do I say?

I know what I am going to say. I have rehearsed these words a thousand times. The pigs have heard me start and restart my words. I have wept over these words. They have broken my heart; and I own them.

'Father'. (Do I have the right to still call him that?) The term 'father' means love, care, guidance, example, and wisdom. I robbed him of those qualities when I left. I heard my pride shout back, 'I can do this alone; I know better,' as I walked towards the horizon. How could He still love me? Is 'Father' too intimate? Should I say 'Sir' or 'Master'? The past relationship that I had with Him is a distant memory, almost a lifetime away.

Surely, the closeness is gone. Even the tone I choose must be formal. I need to show Him I am real. There have been so many times that I felt I needed to go home, but they were fleeting. I just turned back to play; and the Voice got less and less till I had pretty much drowned it out. Busyness, pleasure, hard work, others, quickly replaced the void. It was easy to fill; or so I thought. There were long nights of pain and loneliness. I put on a mask, a happy face to all those around me. They would never have guessed. Surely, I had it all together. But now, I just want Him.

'Father' is right. Nothing else will do, I just want Him. 'Father' speaks of humility. I want to simply be real. Be vulnerable, though every part of me screams out in fear.

'I have sinned against God; I have sinned before You'. I will be open. The truth is the best way. Actually, now it is all I have: it is the only way. I chose to reject His wisdom and to run headlong towards the night. Sin is rebellion. In the other direction, there is a standard: I cannot just live as I like; there are consequences. I have offended God. I have hurt my Father. Words flood in: accountability; confession; take ownership; do not blame. That is my plan. I have no excuses to offer; I am not looking for blessings. He owes me nothing. I will simply appeal to His mercy. My sin haunts me; it is a badge of shame. No one else is to blame. I transgressed His commands, broke His laws, turned away from Him, knelt before the gods of this world, and bathed in iniquity. I am culpable, and honesty is the best policy.

'I do not deserve to be called Your son'. That is so difficult to say aloud. I rejected Him as my Father; I abandoned the family name, and I gave up any rights of sonship. I could not wait for my inheritance; to get what was rightfully mine. I saw only a privilege of sonship, not the responsibility. How did I get this so spectacularly wrong? He had worked so hard for my future, and was freely storing it for me. Worse still, He just freely gave it when I asked so selfishly. There was no discussion; no argument; He just gave it to me, as I walked away from responsibility. The tasks He had planned for me I simply shelved indefinitely. It did not matter to me. I cannot imagine the pain it caused Him; my Father, knowing that I preferred the company of others to His. I wanted to experience the life that others lived; to taste what the world offered. Now, I can almost feel the disappointment. I hurt Him so much that it is better to acknowledge that pain. I have no expectations, but will simply say sorry. I am undeserving; no longer good enough to be recognised as Yours.

I will finish with repentance. I will do anything to be forgiven. Take me on as a hired hand: I can work hard and maybe the years of toil will repay some of what I took from Him. It will be enough just to be in the household; free or slave; I do not mind. Just to be caught up with Him will be reward enough. Maybe eventually I will get a smile or a kind word from Him. It may take time to prove that my repentance is genuine, but I am determined not to let Him down again.

With every step, I am getting closer to home. Fear, excitement, guilt, relief; I am all over the place; but now I know what I will say. He is good; He is love; He is my Father. If it takes the rest of my life to make up for the past, this is my goal. It is better to be near Him than anywhere else. I have been in the darkest places imaginable. To be in His presence will be enough. The world was empty; it did not fill the aching. I feel my steps quicken. I have not once looked back. I have no pang for the past life; I just want to be right with my Father. I want to make Him proud; to see Him smile. I keep going over that first moment I shall see Him. Will He even want me there? Will I hear 'I told you so'? Will He tell me how much of a disappointment I am, compared to my brother? Will He listen? Will He be ashamed of me? Will I see how much I hurt Him? What if He rejects me as I did Him? The enemy is busy.

CHAPTER 6

His past blessing

Not long now. As I walk, I see familiarity. The memories of good times rush back. When I was in that dark place, I could not even remember His presence, nor how He was still working in my life. I would watch others daily: how successful they appeared; new jobs, bigger houses, better holidays, and seemingly impacting the world. Yet, there was I feeding pigs; aching to taste the pods. Famine was raging; I was never satisfied. I had nothing.

I lost perspective. I could not remember times when my Father had helped me. They seemed so insignificant to others' amazing stories. I struggle to remember all the times He was there for me before I left.

As I walk through places I know, I remember more clearly. I remember all the times He provided for me; all the moments of protection; the guidance, the love. He was always there; always listened. He would help me find perspective. He would affirm uniqueness, teaching me that He was enough. I did not need to compare myself with others. Then sin destroyed me in so many ways; emptied my self-esteem;

removed hope. It tore apart the notion that I was unique; that I was special. Life was lonely, and I had no-one to confide in; no one to cry to; no one to listen. He was always for me. He loved me. He accepted me. I took all that He had given to me and that He had put into me, and I had decided it was not enough. Now, in honest, open humility, I am genuinely sorry. I am truly penitent. I was wrong: I cannot live without Him.

My heart is pounding through my chest, and I still have some way to go. What reception will I get? Will it be frosty? Will He make it difficult? Will my words be the correct words to say? Is there a set formula of words to repent? Surely, I admit my sin; it was my choice. I take the full blame; I then humbly confess it. I know I cannot undo the sin nor the consequences to me or others. I broke His ways, and chose my own: the way of the world. I lay it all bare, and hide nothing. I was brought to my knees in that pigsty. It may have been the most difficult time of my life, but it was the moment my conscience was awakened. I am a sinner, and maybe the worst.

I know I cannot make up for it. I caused much hurt both at home and in the city, and now I simply throw myself on the mercy of my Father. I know He loves me, somehow. I do not deserve forgiveness: all I can do is beg. I need to be right with Him. I need His strength not to go back to my sin; His help to resist the urge. I know this will not be easy.

Not long now. Hope is starting to rise. I am close to home. Whatever reaction He gives, this is the right choice. I want to be with Him; to be part of His family and to be home.

CHAPTER 7

My Father's reaction

He ran to me!

I still had the last part of the journey to go, but all I could see was my Father running towards me. He had tears in His eyes. He had a smile; the widest smile I have ever seen! It was all so much to take in. I was tired from the journey; weary from the bad choices that had plagued me since I took my inheritance. I was anxious and fearful. To be honest, I had not even seen Him before that point. I just looked up, and there He was, coming towards me.

The joy on His face melted me. How could He behave like that? I am the sinner; I let Him down. I deserve the consequences. He was waiting for me, and I cannot understand it. My Father, whom I had hurt so badly, was looking for me. How long had He been waiting? How could He still care so much? He does not owe me anything. I am finding it difficult to process. I deserve to be held accountable for my decisions and actions. I betrayed Him; I left Him; I turned my back on Him; I walked towards the bright lights; I spent what He had worked so hard for; and yet, here I am in my Father's embrace. He has not punished me however. He has not admonished me.

Mercy.

Unconditional love.

How could I deserve this? I am ready to acknowledge my sin, and will take whatever punishment He decides. Yet I simply feel His warmth. He is pulling me tighter. As the tears stream down His face, I am broken. I am simply caught up in His presence. I do not want this hug to end. All of my past has disappeared: the fear I felt has gone, and I feel safe. The strength in His arms: how can I explain it?

I have carried a heavy burden of sin, of guilt and shame for so long. I did not like who I saw in the mirror. I was ashamed of myself. He knows me. He knows my failures. Nothing is hidden from my Father. He knows the wrong I have done; the hurt I have caused others; the pain I have put Him through; the damage I caused to the family name – and yet, He is choosing me. I cannot explain it. I have no answers other than He loves me. This is mercy in action. I know what I deserve; I thought I would have to earn His forgiveness. I was ready to work hard as a hired servant;

prove myself to Him; show Him I am repentant; set the scales right – to work hard to outweigh the sin in my life.

Mercy is the withholding of due punishment. I am experiencing mercy. Grace goes further: it is the undeserved favour of my Father. This is mercy and grace rolled into one. I am flabbergasted. I was not expecting this, not even in my wildest dreams. My Father was waiting expectantly for me, the failure. I thought I had walked too far away from His favour; walked away from His love. How can He simply forgive me? How can He accept me, knowing what I have done? I have not even said the words I need to say, which I had all prepared. The guilt is mine; I own it. He kissed me, but I do not deserve the intimacy. He is for me, on my side. I do not deserve it. I am guilty. The world has rejected me, yet He accepts me. He is the one I hurt the most. Love is pouring out of Him. I can feel His heart pounding, bursting through His chest. How long has He waited for me? How did He know I would return? I want to change. I want to be His again.

Minutes ago, I was walking towards home; and now, here I am, in my Father's embrace. There was me thinking it was I who was running to Him, when all the time it was Him who was running to me. Humility ran to me. It was me who was the sinner, yet all I feel is His love. His love is wrapped around me. I have already forgotten who I was before. My heart is jumping for joy. In years, this is the first time I feel secure; the first time I have felt peace. He came to me. I am simply overwhelmed by His response. This is truly amazing grace. How can a wretch like me stand before Him? He made the way and took the initiative. He chose to love. He has made a way when I could not see a way. He is willing to forgive. This is love – a clear demonstration. His actions speak loud and clear. It is not about me; it never was, it was all about who He is, the God who is more than enough.

Woe is me! I am undeserving. He moved when He did not have to. The years I was away have instantly faded. He made it as if the time away never happened. He has brought me home.

CHAPTER 8

What I said, but what He heard

I had it all worked out. It started in the pigsty, and I put the finishing touches to my apology as I walked home. It was perfect. The seriousness of my sin and my rejection of Him as my Father, required a sincere acknowledgement of my guilt. I have been rehearsing it for days: changing words, adjusting the emphasis to make it more meaningful. 'Father, I have sinned against God, I have sinned before You; I do not deserve to be called Your son. Take me on as a hired hand.' I was hoping to kneel before Him in humility, look into His eyes and plead for acceptance; for forgiveness.

I never even got to say what I had rehearsed. It was as if He knew my heart. He did not even give me the opportunity to fall to my knees; to show Him that I was the guilty party. The words were on the tip of my tongue; but He looked right through me deep into my soul. He knew. I cannot explain it, but He just knew. I am convinced that His embrace accepted the words I did not say.

There was no awkward silence. He allowed no moment for me to denigrate myself further. It was as if He knew the journey I had walked. At that moment I felt it so strongly, more strongly than ever, He is for me. The warmth in His face, the tight enveloping of His embrace and the knowing look, took my breath away. I was unable to speak. He never gave me a chance.

How could He have known what had happened to me since I arrogantly walked away from Him? How could He know the shame I brought upon myself? The nights of sin; the shameful situations I found myself in; the sleepless nights; the anger at how I behaved; the overwhelming guilt I felt. And yet I chose to go around the cycle again. How could He know the hurt I caused others? How could He have seen me at my lowest point: envious of the pigs; aching for their food? All those deliberate and degrading acts; the evil words; the unbecoming thoughts and the emptiness. He would not have even recognised me. How could He know?

More so, how could He still care for me and love me unconditionally? Furthermore, how could He just accept me without explanation? This is mercy. I am undeserving. What a wretched man I am, what a wonderful Father! This was a lesson: the greatest lesson. I simply lifted my eyes off the road and looked to Him. He came running. He initiated forgiveness. He made a way when there was no way. He just needed me to come back home. I broke His heart and yet,

His love for me is so great, that He has just brought me back in. This is truly amazing grace!!

I tried to get the words out, but was lost in how He responded. He just knew. It was as if my presence; my being in His arms again, was the point. Somehow, He knew my guilt. He saw it etched on my face by the years of hardness of heart. So long was I unrepentant. Pride ruled my heart, and selfishness dictated every step. He knew my shame. He knew my need for change. He knew I was tired of living that way. He knew I was here to confess; to repent and go forward with Him, and no longer look backwards. No longer to allow those giants to destroy me, and nevertheless to accept my fate. He knew that I thought I was no longer worth it: that I felt of no value. He knew my heart was crying out to be accepted. Every sinew was reaching for Him. Everything inside of me was screaming. The pain was unbearable; but right now, in His arms, it was all gone. I could not see my past nor my future: I just felt peace. He had just rescued me.

CHAPTER 9

Clarity

At that moment, the world changed as I now would see it; I had clarity. The clouds that had surrounded me were gone. Dark shadows that had cast their presence over every activity disappeared. The fear, the doubt, the shame all departed. This encounter with my Father has changed my life. He is good. He is just what I needed. I am His.

It all makes sense - all those years of anxiety; of sin and my endless pursuit for fulfilment. I had looked everywhere: pleasure; money; power; friends; experience. I tried everything. I turned my head to each and every new fad. I had to be there. I had to have it. I was entrapped in the addiction; the moments of needing more, never finding enough. I never was satisfied. I tried the best the world had to offer, and found it unfulfilling.

There was always an aching. I had to stop hiding. I had to run to my Father. He knows me. This is where I was always meant to be.

Home.

Here, with Him.

My acceptance was based on His love: His capacity to restore me, no matter how far I had gone. No matter the words of repentance: it is all about Him.

I do not know what the future holds. For the first time in a long time, I am not worried, because I trust my Father. He will provide all I need. And yet the enemy is trying to attack me. He has succeeded so much in the past, and I allowed his evil power in my life. I believed the devil's lies and his half-truths. I used his suggestions, questioning, whispers, to keep me down. "How could Your God accept you? After all you have done, you are not worth it." Does the devil know about that moment? You know… *that* moment? All *those* moments when God's conviction comes.

The self-doubt has gone: I believe in Him, not in me. Belonging to Him is the reason that I have hope. His strength dispels all the lies of the enemy. It was never about me being good enough. Peace is what I have craved. The guilt raging in my heart has been banished, and my Father has done it. It was not about how hard I worked for His forgiveness: it is simply about grace. This is victory! I no longer need to perform; I can at last be myself. I do not need to pretend or impress anyone.

My Father knows me better than I know myself; and yet, He accepts me, complete with the realisation of where I was in my sin. My acceptance of blame, the longing for better, the decision to come home, the need to restore a broken relationship with my Father and the brokenness. He gave me the freedom to go. He watched me walk away; but He never turned His back. He waited for my return.

The truth struck home at that moment. I am conscious that I did waste so much time. His strength reassures me that those scars, those hurts, and those hard times, all served a purpose. They highlighted a deep yearning within to be with my Father.

He has always been here. He never left. He is the anchor. He is unchanging. He has clearly demonstrated His love and goodness for me. I'm all in!

Clarity surfaces. I know who I am in Him and who He is in me; He is my future, and it is secure.

CHAPTER 10

A new set of clothes

Quickly my Father moved past repentance to restoration. Yes, He accepted my repentance and moved quickly to restore me. He called for a robe, which is a clear sign of acceptance; declaring that I am no longer guilty; outside the family; covered in His righteousness. He has accepted me; accepted my shame, guilt and confession. He has accepted my repentance. He made me clean, chose to forgive, and declared me as a worthy son.

He took the pain. He bore my failures, my sin and my debt. This is grace in action: forgiving the sinner, and restoring someone who hurt Him.

He has granted me a new status – I am free in Him. He bears no grudge. There was no 'I told you so'. I cannot explain it. I am a sinner and completely undeserving. He is patient, kind, and loving. He is all that I am not.

He is the offended party, yet He only gave good to me. The righteousness of the robe speaks publicly to everyone that I am restored, and I am made new. I am justified in His presence; not by anything I had done, but by Him. I deserved punishment, but all I got was love. I deserve condemnation, but He gave grace. There is nothing more powerful than forgiveness. We both were not at fault – only me. I am culpable. Yet, my Father has identified me as clean in His sight. It's called amazing grace!

The robe also speaks of worth. He now recognises me as part of the family, as His son. The son He had lost, but is now found. My identity is now in Him. His name is the one I take on. I am truly home. My rejection is met with acceptance. He has chosen to forgive and forget the hurt I caused. This is overwhelming. It is so difficult to understand. I thought that partial restoration was the first step, then I would have to work my way back into His favour. I was prepared to work for as long as it took to show Him that I am serious about my repentance. No matter what, I was going to prove myself. Yet, He works to a different set of values. They are governed by love. Unconditional love. It is unpredictable. It is active. It is complete. He is love. His character is the source of His actions. He is for me. I cannot understand it. There is no answer to the "why" questions other than that He forgives because He can. He forgives because He loves. He wants a relationship with me – one built on acceptance;

on being right in His eyes; on His initiative and one founded on His ideals. Mercy and grace are two sides of the one coin – and I deserved neither; yet He freely gives.

Finally, the robe signifies protection. He is once again my Father. He commits to protect me. I live inside His house. His walls surround me and protect me from all the dangers and snares out there. The temptation to return to my past sin; the inwardly critical voice that tells me I am not good enough, and the wiles of the enemy: they are no match for my Father. He is bigger than they are. He can and does protect me. I am now where He is. Here is peace. Here is safety. I am accepted.

CHAPTER 11

Significance

He summoned His servants to bring a ring and put it on my finger. This gift goes even further into His heart. He does not just accept me, restore me and protect me; He gives me significance. He is showing the world that I have a position. Everything that is His is now mine. I am an heir once again. I thought that I had stripped all that away when I walked away from Him. Yet, He has restored me; and for the future I am secure. His provision is immeasurable. He owns the cattle on a thousand hills, and He has accepted me. His acceptance has opened the door to sonship. I am not just a servant. We are working to His agenda. He leads, I follow. The joy I feel is incomparable. Even the bright lights of the city pale into insignificance when set against His presence. I feel whole. I had been searching everywhere for meaning; for satisfaction; and for purpose; now in my Father, I have found them. Nothing else will do.

The ring bestows authority. It is not just a sign of a relationship with my Father. It is concerned with power. He empowers me to impact the world. In Him, my past is forgotten. My sin is forgiven. My enemy is defeated. I am strong in Him. In the past, I was at war with myself. My foes were many: including myself, my enemy and the world. They were constantly pulling me away from Him; and also away from who I was in Him. My identity was undermined. The power disappeared; I was unable to overcome. My conscience was numbed by the lust of the world in that season of life. I was lost.

The ring gives authority over loneliness; insignificance; finding myself wanting; my worthlessness; sin; guilt; the foes and the shame: they are all defeated. The disappointment was the hardest emotion to cope with. Hating myself for my poverty; my bad choices; the hurt I had willingly caused Him; and the inability to do anything about it. The addictive tendencies, fed by the power of the enemy, were intoxicating. This ring grants me value. It gives me a new identity. The shadow is gone. There is mercy for me now that I am a new man. I am filled with joy! He waited for the one: for me. His love is limitless. His love is extravagant: not only pardoning me but restoring me. He empowers me. He gave me beyond what I had forfeited. I can approach Him freely. I can call on Him anytime, every time. There is nothing He cannot do for me. I now live in His grace; His timing; and His plan. He rejoices over me. He whispers to me that He is proud of me. I do not need to tell Him how far I fell; He knows. He never considered how much He would lose for me. He just ran to me. He is not cautious. He is all in. He gives me all things. He gives Himself to me again and again and again. His patience is limitless. He has my heart: all of me. He accepts me. He deserves all of me. I freely choose Him because He chose me.

Then there is the feast. He goes beyond, every time. His exact words were: 'Then get a grain-fed heifer and roast it. We are going to feast! We are going to have a wonderful time!' How do I even deserve this? Feasting is about honouring. Feasting is about celebrating. His ways are not my ways. The shame I brought to Him is real. I can only imagine the hurt. Yet, He is rejoicing that I am alive; that I am found. The best of the cattle is sacrificed for me. He centres in on people; possessions mean nothing to Him. The expressions of His love are boundless: a robe; a ring; and a feast. I am just thankful. I do not even have the words to thank Him. I just need to accept His rich love. When I consider the phrase that He used – the term He uses – 'We', 'Together,' 'He and I.' I am no longer alone; I am back where He believes I belong.

CHAPTER 12

Purpose

When I was there feeding pigs, I thought that was the end. I was useless to everyone, and had no right to expect to have purpose. No matter what educational achievements I have; what experience in business; what sparkling personality; what strengths I have; or what great references I carry; the bottom-line is, I ended up feeding pigs which was against everything my Father desired.

On the face of it, the very fact my Father asked His servants to bring me a pair of sandals seems irrelevant. It seems merely to replace the bare-footed walking. Comfort for my pain; but it is much more than that. He knows I want to have meaning. He has restored my identity as a son; now He knows I want to be His son. In a way, He is helping me discover my strengths. He is giving me an opportunity to find somewhere to serve in the family kingdom business that fits who I am. I want to live for this bigger ideal – His purpose.

He wants me to take my new-found freedom – freedom that His righteousness has granted – and be busy for Him. He knows that I will find deeper fulfilment being with Him and serving His purpose. His plan He has for me will be better than what I imagine. He knows me better than I know myself. He can read my facial expressions; my mood swings; my disappointment. He knows what excites me. He knows how to ignite my interest. I am forever indebted to Him, so I will give Him everything. I will serve; I will follow, gladly letting Him lead. He will decide my next steps. I was headstrong and sowed the seeds of my destruction. Left to my own devices, I get into trouble. I need the accountability of my Father in my life. I need His presence. I want to become closer to Him. I do want to work hard for Him. My standing was not changed because of anything I did. He declared me forgiven, accepted and restored by His actions. Knowing that He forgave my sin; the pain I caused; my lack of guilt; my cycle of addiction and the endless desire for more, humbles me. He chose me; He has rescued me.

The experiences that I have been through have shaped me. Being lost but now found; effectively dead, but now alive. These experiences have given me a sense of purpose. I want to tell the world how great my Father is. I want to praise publicly and acknowledge all that He has done for me. It is all about Him. My journey back is really His journey. He reluctantly let me walk away. He allowed me to pursue my desires, though it hurt Him deeply. He waited daily and patiently for my return. He initiated acceptance in running to forgive me. He restored me. He declared me clean in His eyes, and He has given me an opportunity to have meaning, significance and purpose. I will tell everyone who will listen, and even those who will not listen. Everyone needs to hear how wonderful my Father is; how big His heart is; how unconditional and strong is His love. I do not know at this moment what purpose He has for me – big or small; public or private; in or out of my comfort zone. All I know is I am willing to do what He asks. I have experienced what this broken world offers. I knew emptiness. I knew shame. Now, I know acceptance. I know real love.

I belong to my Father. He has found me. Hallelujah!

And You?

Can I ask… Do you want to come home? The wasted years can be restored to you. God wants you. You are never too far away to come home. God can forgive all things, no matter what they are, when we come to Him and are truly repentant. Are you ready to return to Him now?

Let me pray with you…

Dear Lord Jesus,
I want to know You personally.
I am sorry for going my own way instead of Your way.
Thank you for dying on the cross to forgive my sins.
Please come and take first place in my life and make me the person You want me to be.
Bring me onto the path home.

Amen

The context of this story is found in Luke 15:11-24…

"Then he said, "There was once a man who had two sons. The younger said to his father, 'Father, I want right now what's coming to me.' It was not long before the younger son packed his bags and left for a distant country. There, undisciplined and dissipated, he wasted everything he had.

"After he had gone through all his money, there was a bad famine all through that country and he began to hurt. He signed on with a citizen there who assigned him to his fields to slop the pigs. He was so hungry he would have eaten the corncobs in the pig slop, but no one would give him any.

"That brought him to his senses. He said, 'All those farmhands working for my father sit down to three meals a day, and here I am starving to death. I am going back to my father. I will say to him, "Father, I have sinned against God, I have sinned before you; I do not deserve to be called your son. Take me on as a hired hand." He got right up and went home to his father.

"When he was still a long way off, his father saw him. His heart pounding, he ran out, embraced him, and kissed him. The son started his speech: 'Father, I've sinned against God, I've sinned before you; I don't deserve to be called your son ever again.'

But the father wasn't listening. He was calling to the servants, 'Quick. Bring a clean set of clothes and dress him. Put the family ring on his finger and sandals on his feet. Then get a grain-fed heifer and roast it. We are going to feast! We are going to have a wonderful time! My son is here - given up for dead and now alive! Given up for lost and now found!' And they began to have a wonderful time." The Message

Contact the author by emailing

g.cowie.writing@outlook.com

Inspired to write a book?

Contact

Maurice Wylie Media

Inspirational Christian Publisher

Based in Northern Ireland and distributing around the world.

www.MauriceWylieMedia.com